We Spent
Half Our Lives on the
Wrong Side
of the Road

OUR STORY READS
LIKE A NICE
ROUND OF GOLF

ENJOY

[signature]

Ron Kirby

We Spent
Half Our Lives on the
Wrong Side
of the Road

With a Forward by Jack Nicklaus

Charleston, SC
www.PalmettoPublishing.com

We Spent Half Our Lives on the Wrong Side of the Road

Hardcover ISBN: 978-1-64990-811-7
Paperback ISBN: 978-1-64990-955-8

To Sally,

It began with chop suey sandwiches at Salem Willows Park, our regular date after I picked you up from work at the dress shop. You were the most polite, caring person, and you always looked smashing, thanks in part to those charge accounts you had at the local dress shops. We would sit on the grass and dream of our future

Sally and Ron, two sweethearts at Quincy Park, Beverly, Massachussets

together. The life we envisioned for ourselves in those days was nothing like the life we lived and enjoyed for over sixty-seven years.

I dedicate this book to you, Sally. Thank you for choosing me, helping with career decisions, making the places we lived homes, being the most caring and loving mother to our children, grandchildren, and great-grandchildren, and last but not least, being the one to lead and develop the hundreds of friendships we had worldwide. God blessed me when He gave you to me. Now He wants you back. I miss you so much!

Love,
Ron

Jack Nicklaus, Sally and Ron in Ponte Vedra at ASGCA meeting

Forward

I have always said, if not preached, that people are truly successful only at the things they truly love. If there is one person who I have been blessed to know over my lifetime who built a storied career because of an unwavering love for the game of golf, it is Ron Kirby. Ron doesn't just love playing the game of golf, he loves everything there is about the game—from the design of courses, construction of them, the maintenance of golf facilities, and yes, the playing of them. Ron could never get enough of this great game, and because of it, he has left a little piece of himself in every facet of it and in every corner of the world.

Much like I am fortunate to say about my own life, the game of golf has taken Ron around the globe, and I think he will tell you that his life has been made rich or richer because of it.

Here is someone who, in the early 1960s while working in The Bahamas, played golf with then former Vice President Richard Nixon and The Tonight Show host Jack Paar, and then had them over to watch Paar on TV, as his wife Sally served cookies and coffee. Fast-forward to the 1970s and Ron, while on a construction visit in North Carolina, was hunted down to take a phone call from the famous Imelda Marcos—wife of the President of The Philippines—because she wanted to ask Ron if he could build a golf course as a gift for her husband's 60th birthday…in three months!

And then there was the late 1980s, when Ron came to work for me as a full-time designer. Next thing you know, Ron was moving his family from Atlanta to Monaco to London, doing design work all over Europe, where he found himself on site visits with everyone from a Golden Bear to 007—the late Sean Connery.

Of all the different countries and places the game of golf took him, one thing always remained the same— Ron. There are not many people I have met over the course of my life as nice, as easy-going, and as likable as Ron Kirby. The same could be said for his wonderful late wife Sally. I think Ron's personality and demeanor are what attracted me to him, as much as his talent and love for the game. He was wonderful with clients, and the example he set for the younger designers we had around the world—some of whom are still with me many decades later—is why Ron Kirby is a special person to me and so many others.

I could probably tell you countless stories of Ron, but I will allow him to do that in the following pages. But I think even Ron might agree that more important than the places we visited and the courses we designed are the quiet times we spent—perhaps just fishing the flats in The Bahamas—simply talking about life. And for Ron, it's been a life well played!

Good golfing,
Jack Nicklaus

Gary Larrabee & Ron at Hall of Fame Award

Sally trying hard to write our story on a cruise

Preface

S ally and I had always planned to write a book about our life story. Since 1950, no one can argue that our lives were not filled with adventure. I am incredibly grateful for my golf design career, which enabled us to travel to many countries and make lasting friendships all over the world. The goal of this book is not to be something mass-produced, but rather to write a story that our children, grandchildren, great-grandchildren, and friends can read and enjoy.

Gary Larrabee, a longtime friend and golf writer from Wenham, Massachusetts, routinely encouraged Sally and me over the years to begin writing our book. Gary has always been a big supporter of my golf career, and he is a big reason I was inducted into the Beverly, Massachusetts High School Hall of Fame. In 2014 Gary traveled to Ireland to tour my golf courses. Upon our return, he advised Sally and me to get our notes down on paper—anything that would document our life journey together.

We began writing our notes during a couple of our transatlantic cruises and flew to Boston to meet with

Gary and his wife, Anne, to get the project underway. However, life got in the way, whether it was additional design projects or health issues; thus, the project too often found itself placed on the back burner.

Now, with Sally at rest, it is time to complete the story on my own the best I can with the help of Gary and my daughter Beverly. The book is organized according to where Sally and I were living at that period in time. Having lived in eighteen homes, you can say we enjoyed a full round of golf.

Part One

THE FRONT NINE

15 AND 13 MULBERRY ST
BEVERLY, MASS

1st Hole

13-15 MULBERRY STREET

BEVERLY, MASSACHUSETTS

These early days in Beverly are memories of my brother, Bill, and me growing up, doing all the normal things young brothers do—pick-up sand lot baseball, our own basketball hoop at the shop, caddy jobs, pin setting in the bowling alleys at the United Shoe Country Club and the Beverly YMCA, and pond ice hockey at the United Shoe pond in the winter.

I attended Washington Elementary and Briscoe Junior High, graduated from Beverly High School, class of 1950. My grandparents were Nan and William

Wallace (WW) Crosby, who lived in Number 15 Mulberry Street with my mother, Ethel, living next door at 13 Mulberry Street.

My parents divorced in the mid-1940s when I was ten years old, and my father, Paul Kirby (PK), moved to New Hampshire to become a golf professional. My mom, Ethel (Mimi), continued to live on Mulberry Street and worked as a waitress at Moe's Restaurant in Peabody. To many, she was considered a fixture there. She drove a fancy Buick, and that was important to her. It should be noted that she would drive Buicks the rest of her life. As a single mom, she did the best she could, raising two active sons in sports.

Through the caddy years and high school, golf became a major part of our lives. Bill and I played on the high school golf team. It can be said that young boys playing golf in Beverly in the '40s and '50s would be unusual for sure. Two things happened to set this course for the future.

My grandfather's painting company was awarded the contract to re-paint the clubhouse at the Kernwood Country Club in Salem, Massachusetts. During this assignment, the golf professional gave my grandfather a set of golf clubs. In the 1920s, he joined a group that had founded in 1899 a new golf course named Wenham Golf Club. The second thing that happened in the late 1920s–early 1930s, my dad, Paul Kirby, club champion at Wenham Golf Club, married Ethel Crosby, the daughter of one of the Wenham GC founders.

So, golf in my early years was not unusual at all, which led me along the path of becoming a caddy master and securing golf course maintenance positions while in high school. I eventually went to turf school at the University of Massachusetts with the help of a Francis Ouimet Caddy Scholarship in 1950, an honor of which I am very proud and continue to support to this day. In my early years I also liked to visit my grandfather and paint. From this interest came my winter Saturday morning art classes at the Boston Museum of Fine Arts. I learned skills and techniques at the MFA that have helped me greatly as a golf course designer.

Ethel (Mimi) and Paul (PK) – Ron's Mom and Dad

PK at lesson tee

Sally - High School Photo

Anna Williams - Sally's mom

26 Fossa Terrace
Beverly Mass

2nd Hole

26 Fossa Terrace

Beverly, Massachusetts

S ally was the youngest of seven children (two boys and five girls) of Chet and Anna Williams. When I met Sally in 1949, she and her sister June were the last daughters living at home. We met through our friend Fran, who I was dating at the time. When things ended between Fran and me, I asked her if it would be okay for me to ask Sally out on a date, and she actually encouraged this. Our first date was to Salem Willows, where we enjoyed a nice stroll at the park and a chop suey sandwich . . . and the rest is history, as it is said. To say Sally was the pretty one does not come close to describing her. She was beautiful in appearance, politeness, and thoughtfulness, which made her stand out anywhere she went. She loved nice clothes and had charge accounts with many nice stores in Salem. Often, Sally was working at the drug store, at Kennedy's butter and eggs store, and part-time as a telephone operator. Later, after Sally and her mom moved to Fitchburg to be closer to her sister Vi and her husband, Bud, she got a nice job at Foster Grant. She always dressed up so perfectly when we had a date. Sally was asked to be a contestant for the "Miss Beverly at the Beach" contest in 1950 and won! For sure, Sally had a few boyfriends after high school, but she liked me best, which explains why we married in 1952.

Sally in Miss Beverly Beach Pageant

Ron and Sally wedding - 1952

Ron and Sally with Vi and Ethel (Mimi) at wedding, 1952

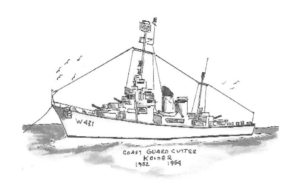

COAST GUARD CUTTER
KOINER
1952 1954

W 481

3rd Hole

USCG Cutter

Koiner

1952-1954

Our Coast Guard chapter begins with my decision to leave turf school at UMass due to my draft status classification becoming 1-A, which I received early in my second and final year at school. After receiving a lot of advice, I decided it was best to leave school and join the Coast Guard. Actually, many friends were faced with a similar decision to make. As it happened, six out of nine applicants went off to boot camp in Cape May, New Jersey, on November 19, 1951.

My first assignment was a weather ship, the U.S. Coast Guard *Duane,* based in Boston. After four months, I was transferred to Radar School in Groton, Connecticut. Upon graduating Radar School, Sally and I were married in Beverly, as noted earlier, and I was transferred to the U.S. Coast Guard Cutter *Koiner,* based in Seattle, Washington.

Our years in the Coast Guard featured our maturing and growing as married adults on a fast track. Sally found a place for us to rent for free. Sally had to clean a doctor's office in trade for a room in the lower level of an apartment of a big house. This was a great help since we were receiving about one hundred dollars per month as a married seaman and wife. Later, Sally found another apartment and got a job at Fredrick Nelson's department store in downtown Seattle. At the same time, Sally was pregnant with our first daughter, Faye. Shipboard life was challenging, but a promotion to Third Class Petty Officer was a good jump that helped with living expenses.

The normal schedule for our ship was out to sea for about forty days followed with duty in the port of Seattle for the same amount of time. Each ship had to also take a six-month trip out through Midway, Guam, Japan, and Alaska once every two years. Sally was due with Faye during one of these long trips, so Sally and

I joined another shipmate and his wife who was also pregnant, and we went back to Beverly. Sally stayed and gave birth to Faye at Beverly Hospital, and I returned west for the six-month trip on the *Koiner*.

Faye arrived on March 26, 1953. My appendix burst at sea off Alaska in July that summer. After surgery in Kodiak, Alaska, they transferred me to a hospital in Seattle where I first met my darling daughter Faye. After a couple of months of sick leave, I went back to sea on the *Koiner*.

With a little bit of luck, and Sally putting our names on a waiting list for Navy housing, we got a really nice end unit apartment at Sand Point Naval Housing. This is how Sally shined, making friends and developing a true family life, especially when Ron Jr. came along on September 26, 1954 at the Army base in Fort Lawton.

Later that fall, my mother, Ethel (Mimi), flew out to Seattle to help with our journey back east in our small Nash Rambler. Saying goodbye to our neighbors and friends at the ship was sad, but Sally managed to keep up with some of them over the years. Lucy Foley is one of those friends we visited a few years ago in Lodi, California.

I had a good friend from high school named Art Collins, who joined the Coast Guard at the same time I did in1951, during the Korean War conflict. Art Collins was the best man at our wedding and later became godfather to Ron Jr. when we returned from Seattle.

Art and I kept in contact with each other often after the Coast Guard years. He was a true Beverly native and ended up having a career at City Hall.

Our next stops would be short ones. It was transition time back to school at UMass.

Ron's Shipmates on the Koiner

Emergency Evacuation in Alaska for Appendix

PRO SHOP & HOUSE
PETERSHAM
COUNTRY CLUB

4th Hole

PETERSHAM COUNTRY CLUB

1957-1959

The transition from our Coast Guard years in Seattle to civilian life in Beverly took a few years before our goals were reset, and I went back and finished school at UMass, Stockbridge Turf College. During the winter of 1957, I interviewed with a few golf courses in New England for both assistant and head greenskeeper positions.

Securing the Pro Greenskeeper position at Petersham Country Club (PCC) was a perfect match for

Sally and me. It was a nine-hole established course in central Massachusetts. Duties comprised course maintenance with two retired workers, pro shop operations including tournaments and events, along with clubhouse maintenance. Additionally, Sally on occasion provided Sunday breakfast for the directors.

Having lived in the married dorms at UMass/ Amherst on the G.I. bill, this position was a blessing. We were hired early in the winter, and with a lot of help from Sally's sister Vi and her husband, Bud, we got the house livable by spring. The course was ready to open by early May for the members.

The years at Petersham were challenging but fun because the members were really nice to our family. We were staff, but even more, so the members became new friends. The club had about one hundred members and the usual committees to organize and schedule golf events, control handicaps and rules, and handle social events throughout the season. We joined all the member activities and truly loved the club and friends.

Petersham is a small town close to Athol, a bit farther north from Ware and Brookfield, towns from where members hailed in the Greater Worcester area. The Union Twist Drill Company in Athol was a main financial benefactor of the club. Their directors and board members were Petersham directors and board members. When we were hired at PCC, it was agreed that I would work in the factory during the winter months, though the club had plans for a curling rink in the future. Eventually the club did build the curling rink, yet for the three winters we traveled south to Miami in search of temporary golf course work.

My dad was most helpful during this period, introducing me to Mark Mahanah, a golf course architect, and others involved in course construction. Faye and Ron Jr. were just beginning school, so we were able to make this work, but soon it would be impossible to pick up and leave every winter.

Golf at Petersham was very good for both Sally and me. I played in all the men's events and established a handicap. Sally began to play and had three girlfriends who wanted to learn. They played early in the morning, had a lot of laughs, and enjoyed being alone on the course. They all became nice players. One in the group became the lady's club champion. Sally played local lady events at other clubs and held her own.

Across from the club entrance was Harry and Fran Kuniholm's house. Harry had a jewelry store in Athol where Sally worked part-time, and Fran became Sally's life-long friend. Sally loved to dress up and meet people. Another house by the club was the Kelly's, whose young boy, Charlie Kelly, became part of our team, watching the pro shop and babysitting. He wanted to be on the course as much as possible. Charlie learned to play golf nicely, displayed great manners, and went on to be a doctor in New York.

The three seasons at Petersham gave us three winters in South Florida. Each winter, opportunities for golf projects increased. During the winter of 1959-60 we went to Nassau to interview for the head greenskeeper position at Bahamas Country Club. This was the next big step in our lives, and we gave it a lot of thought in regards to what we wanted life for our family to look like. It helped so much that Millie and Al Collins, the golf pro and his wife at the Bahamas Country Club and Sleepy Hollow in New York, gave us valuable counsel as we were deciding our future. We accepted the position in Nassau and went back immediately that winter to advise the club directors at Petersham Country Club that we would not be coming back for the spring of 1960. Not an easy task for either of us, but it had to happen. It would be a big change from Petersham Country Club to Bahamas Country Club.

PARADICE ISLAND
NASSAU BAHAMAS

5th Hole

PARADISE ISLAND

(Note: Remember to drive on the left)

1960-1963

The three years in the Bahamas were actually two different assignments. First was a renovation at Bahamas Country Club (BCC), an old course on the main island of Nassau. The second project was a completely new construction of an 18-hole resort course across the bay from Nassau on Paradise Island.

Sally and I, along with Faye and Ron Jr., began our stay at Bahamas Country Club, sharing a suite of rooms at the beachfront hotel, dining with the hotel staff. This was difficult in many ways; luckily, we got much better living arrangements thanks to Sally and the owner, Lady Oaks. They built an apartment for us above the men's and ladies' locker rooms; it was very nice and convenient—small, but with first-class views of the sea.

My assignment at BCC was to redo all eighteen greens, tees, and all bunkers, as well as install a new irrigation system using recycled water from neighboring hotels. This was a huge and complicated project; learning on the job was a demanding test. Sally was hired to meet and greet golfers at the front desk of the golf club, once again a perfect fit.

Across from our new apartment was the apartment of Millie and Al Collins, the club professional. Millie and Sally became close friends, and Al and I developed a similar friendship. I would watch over the pro shop operations during the summer when Millie and Al left to travel. Another friendship came about with Anna and Butch Carey. Anna worked at the Bahamas Country Club in the main hotel office. Butch was a boat person, supervising maintenance for large boats in Nassau. Butch helped me with a lot of mechanical and irrigation items at the course. We became close, personal family friends, celebrating holidays and birthdays, hosting and attending many parties.

During our time at the Bahamas Country Club, the news about the new course at Paradise Island got around town. Fortunately, I received a tour of the island project and decided this would be a special development, and I should put my name into the mix to be a part of it. My efforts at Bahamas Country Club did get results. Once the renovated greens and irrigation work was completed, this project's results helped me in getting assigned to grow in the course at Paradise Island for the Ocean Club.

I had met with Dick Wilson's design team in Florida and made it known to them that I would like to be part of their project at Paradise Island when an opening for a greenskeeper surfaced. It took a few months, but the greenskeeper's house was designed by the same Ocean Club team of architects and designers; the cottage was really nice.

Living out on the course at Paradise Island was an adventure. Faye and Ron Jr. traveled by boat to school each day. Sally did as well, getting a front desk office job in the main office for the Ocean Club in Nassau.

Progress was slow for growing in the turf for eighteen holes, but we did manage to get nine holes open for play and completed the golf pro shop. At this stage, the owner hired rising PGA Tour star Gary Player as the touring professional to play and reside at the club. Gary, his wife, Vivienne, and their three children arrived in 1961 to Paradise Island.

The Ocean Club, a fifty-two-room luxury hotel, opened along with the Café Martinique at Hurricane

Hole Marina, but at that time, the population of the island was limited to the local staff, which included the families of myself and Sally, Gary and Vivian Player, Pancho Gonzales, the tennis professional, and Karl Schmidt, the head landscaper. Paradise truly was the proper name for the island.

The golf course grow-in struggled because the fill for some of the holes was dredged from the sea bottom, and we had to leach out the salt before grass could develop on the turf. My friend Al Collins from the Bahamas Country Club called me one day to advise that Robert Trent Jones, the golf course architect of note, was dining at the club and invited me to meet him. It was a great evening, and we discussed my status growing grass on salt-filled areas at Paradise Island. We parted with Mr. Jones giving me his business card and asking me to call him when the entire course was completely grassed.

There were many highlights during our time in Paradise Island. Below are some of the classics.

1. Gary Player tells me that Jack Nicklaus is coming to visit. Not to play golf, but to fish. He wants me to arrange this event. Butch Carey helps, and we get the best boat, best bait, and best captain for his fishing trip. This trip was great for Jack and me; we talked golf design while others slept. To this day, Jack remembers this visit.

2. Al Collins calls me to play with him and a group of VIPs with former Vice-President Richard Nixon. Nixon was staying at the Ocean Club. During the golf game with Nixon, I mentioned I had TV reception from Miami. Jack Paar was playing and told Nixon he had recorded Teddy Kennedy on the show that would air in a couple of nights. It was arranged for the entire Nixon group to come to our house and watch Paar watch Paar. Sally made cookies and coffee, and everyone loved the evening. Later, they put this story in *Newsweek Magazine*.
3. Faye and Ron Jr. met Ricky Nelson, heartthrob, rock and roll star, and son of Ozzie and Harriet, on the boat back to the island. His family was staying at the Ocean Club.

Later that year, I placed a call to Mr. Jones's office in New York City, advising I would be back in Boston in June for the U.S. Open at the Country Club in Brookline. The championship was going to celebrate the 50-year anniversary of Francis Quimet winning the U.S. Open in 1913 as an amateur. All Quimet Caddy Scholarship winners were invited to attend a champions' dinner in Boston during the event, and as a former Ouimet scholar, I was able to make it.

During the trip with my family to Boston and Beverly, I was able to meet Mr. Jones in New York City and was hired to travel and work with his company beginning in September of that year. We returned from the Boston area and made plans to move to Ft. Lauderdale and begin the next chapter of our lives.

Sally with Al and Millie Collins in Nassau

Sally and Ron with Butch and Anna Carey in Nassau

PLANTATION FLORIDA

6th Hole

Plantation

1963-1968

S ally, Ron Jr., and Faye flew out of Nassau on a morning Bahamas Airways flight, and I followed by boat, setting sail out of Paradise Island on the Wando River, the little freighter that we used for getting goods to and from the island. I had our Labrador retriever, Tracy, with me. The captain and crew had a few bottles of champagne with them. With the Bahamas behind us, we were now in Plantation, Florida.

This career move was a big break for me. It was my chance to work for an internationally renowned designer,

Robert Trent Jones. He was known to friends and clients as "Trent Jones," but the staff referred to him as "Mr. Jones." Sally had made a couple of early trips over to the mainland to select a home for us and a school for the kids.

The kids were enrolled in St. Gregory's Catholic school and settled in nicely, wearing school uniforms and riding their bicycles with new friends. It should be noted that Ron Jr. recently reminded me that he would have loved spending his summer vacation with his friends, but I had him enrolled in Caddy Camp at the mountainous Oglebay Park Golf Course in Wheeling, West Virginia the summer of 1966.   Ron Jr. said to me, "Nice Dad, most kids got to relax at the beach; I got to go to Caddy Camp carrying double bags for my summer break."   Sally quickly made friends with the neighbors, which was very helpful because I was doing a lot of traveling for Mr. Jones. I could be gone from the family for months at a time.

One of the first projects I had with Mr. Jones was in late 1963 in San Diego at a course in Tecolote Canyon. This job was very demanding, and during this time there was a great sadness in America and the world because President Kennedy had been assassinated. There was a mourning period when things were closed, and I was only able to call home on Sunday nights. I didn't like being away from home so long; it was a big change in our lifestyle because in the Bahamas I was home every night. In December I decided to speak with Mr. Jones and tell him I was sorry, but this arrangement wasn't working out for us. It was during this conversation that

Mr. Jones advised he could use me at the Mauna Kea, Hawaii project. He assured me he saw a big future for me and asked me to go out to Mauna Kea for six months and to make plans for Sally to join me for a month. When I told Sally about this, she had a big smile on her face and agreed we should take this deal and see where it leads. Vi and Bud took care of the kids while she visited.

The Mauna Kea project moved along nicely. Shortly after Sally returned home, she had to break the news to me that my brother, Bill, had been killed in a car accident outside Boston. I left Hawaii to head back to Boston where Sally met me along with my mother Ethel, PK, and his wife Alice. The funeral was very sad as Bill left behind his wife, Joan, and three children. His family had had all sorts of health problems, including polio.

It was on the flight back from Boston, while reflecting on Bill's sudden death, that Sally and I decided to have another child. We felt it was not the best approach to just have two children because if something tragic happened to one, the other would be all alone. Soon after, on January 11, 1965, Beverly was born at Broward General Hospital in Plantation, Florida. In addition, my mom, Ethel, decided to move to South Florida after Bill's death. She lived with us in Plantation for a short period of time before moving into a Hillcrest Condominium in Hollywood, Florida where she would live the rest of her life.

I continued to work on many projects for Mr. Jones, not only in Hawaii, but also in Puerto Rico, Atlanta, and

West Virginia. I went wherever he saw value in having me, but at least I was able to be home every weekend. That made for a good arrangement for Sally and me. Sally continued to make new friends and eventually started playing golf at Coral Ridge Golf Club. Life was good in Plantation.

It should also be noted that during this time Mr. Jones had a small Fort Lauderdale office in the pro shop at the American Golf Club. He and I had many meetings there; during one of these meetings, he indicated there were irrigation issues at one of his projects in Colorado, the Broadmoor Resort. He said he needed someone who could fix these problems. It was at this meeting that I told him about my brother-in-law, Bud Sexten. I told him Bud would be the right guy to send to the Broadmoor. Mr. Jones agreed, and Bud joined the company working for Jones his entire career and becoming a reliable part of Mr. Jones's and son Bobby Jones's golf course architecture empires.

Countless meetings with Mr. Jones were conducted in airports while we traveled together. It was not uncommon for schedules to change due to weather at sites and various delays at projects. Often, we would be in an airport looking at our individual OAGs (Official Airline Guide) to put a new travel plan in play. There were just so many projects, leads, and courses that needed him.

Another big break for us came when I was traveling with Mr. Jones, and he learned I had a passport. He promptly asked me to represent him at meetings with land planners in Sardinia and Rome regarding a project at Costa Smerelda, Puerto Cervo. Mr. Jones was impressed with how I handled these meetings, leading him to ask me to take the family and move to Europe for a couple of years to be his representative on all his European projects. I gladly accepted.

I had been doing a lot of travel for Mr. Jones in the southeastern United States. I formed close personal contacts through work on projects specifically in and around Georgia and South Carolina. These relationships would come into play upon my return from Europe a few years later. We made the decision to keep the house in Plantation and rent it while we were gone. Rather than fly to Europe, we decide to set sail on a cruise ship from Fort Lauderdale to Southampton by way of Bermuda. It would be the start of an adventure for the whole family.

Ron, Brooks Wigginton, Earl Gaylor, Robert Trent Jones - 1967

PANAL ASH RD
NARROGATE
ENGLAND

7th Hole

PANAL ASH ROAD

(Note: Remember to drive on the left)

HARROGATE, YORKSHIRE, ENGLAND

1963-1968

We arrived in Southampton, England on the *Oriana* cruise ship. We drove to Harrogate to our rented house on Panal Ash Road. Our overseas adventure was all ahead of us. The house and town were wonderful. School for Faye was a convent school, but Ron Jr's arrangements were not the best due to his age, yet he got by at the local comprehensive school.

The projects and travel were exciting and challenging. The main project, Moor Allerton Golf Club, was just a few miles away near Leeds. The Golf Club was relocating—selling the existing 18-hole course and building a new 27-holes and clubhouse nearby. The old greenskeeper at the existing course was George Geddes, who worked with Alister Mackenzie to build the original course, while his son Colin was assigned as greenskeeper for the new course. Colin, his wife, Pauline, and their daughter, Janine, become dear friends. They made the transition to living abroad such a wonderful and exciting time in our lives, continuing through our future life and travels.

Life in Britain was different from life in the United States. Everything was quainter and pleasing; we loved it. The television was much better, and Sally fit in nicely with the neighbors. Life was good, but the schools were marginal in our estimation. My design work was fine, and travel was fun—to a point. The projects, however, were very stimulating. I frequently joined Mr. Jones and his associate in business, Baron Paul Rolan from Belgium, for travel. Mr. Jones was the designer for 18 holes in Belgium for Paul Rolan's brother, and Paul became the head of a golf construction company for all of Mr. Jones' projects in Europe.

Ron Jr. and I played golf on weekend trips to famous links courses in Great Britain. In July 1968, Ron Jr, Faye, and I traveled to Carnoustie to watch Gary Player compete in the British Open while Sally stayed home with Beverly. The three of us stayed in a small pub hotel close to the course, and, by wonderful timing, enjoyed an evening meal with Gary and Vivienne the night before he won the Open championship. This was the first British Open I attended, the first of many I would enjoy with friends and family.

We spent many long daylight evenings with Colin and Pauline, going to the horse races and the Squinting Cat, a local pub in Harrogate with our favorite fruit machine. Colin and Pauline lived nearby in Leeds and managed a green grocery store there. Colin went to the main market every morning to get fresh vegetables, flowers, and fish for the green market before he headed to work at the golf course. Colin and Pauline took Sally and me under their wings and made our lives so much fuller.

We faced one major dilemma. The schools became a problem for Faye and Ron Jr.: we needed to make a change. My design travel often took me to Geneva during the school months. In discussion with friends and after doing a bit of research, we realized an international high school would be best for both of them. We decided to move from Harrogate to Geneva and enroll Faye and Ron Jr. in the International School at Versoix,

College, du Leman. It proved to be a wise choice. Faye and Ron Jr. took a bus from our apartment in town to school just north along the lake. After a few months, we decided to have Faye and Ron Jr. board at the school while Sally, Beverly, and I temporarily moved to a new project in Rabat, Morocco. Once completed, we moved back to Yorkshire to finish the Moor Allerton project in the spring of 1969.

Sally, Bev, Ron Jr. and Faye on board cruise
ship passing White Cliffs of Dover

8th Hole

ROCK HOUSE

(Note: Remember to drive on the left)

SICKLING HALL, YORKSHIRE, ENGLAND

1969

With Faye and Ron Jr. boarding at school in Switzerland, Sally, Beverly, and I went to Rabat, Morocco to live for a few months with the team working on the new course at Royal Golf, Dar Es Salam. The house we had was huge, gated, with staff and a driver. It was an interesting and challenging experience for all of us. Side trips to Marrakesh and Fez were fun, but with good weather we returned to Yorkshire. This time our residence would be Rock House.

The friends we had made during our stay in Harrogate and the new ones we made while at Rock House made this summer in England most memorable. We played golf at Panal Golf Club, took weekend road trips to Scotland, and attended another British Open at Royal Lytham and St. Annes. Those were just a few things that made for a wonderful family summer. In fact, it became tradition; each year Pauline, Colin's wife, would arrange for our group to attend the British Open. From farms in Turnberry for Troon, to Fish & Chips apartments in Sandwich, we have been to more than twenty British Opens.

Ron Jr. had a moped in Geneva, which we sent back to England; it was fun to drive on back lane English roads. Beverly attended kindergarten at the village school; her friends would come along in the morning and walk her to school every day. The projects were moving along nicely, the new course at Moor Allerton was finishing up construction, and the grow-in phase began with Colin in the lead. Colin had found us a Tatter's pony named Flash that lived in the yard at Rock House for the summer. When we returned to Florida in the fall, the village adopted Flash.

Based on project priorities, I will list here the ongoing sites active with Robert Trent Jones during the years 1968 and 1969.

1. Costa Smerelda, Sardinia, Italy (18 holes)
2. Dar Es Salam, Rabat Monaco (27 holes)

3. Club De Golf, Geneva Switzerland (18 holes)
4. Lake Constance, Germany (18 holes)
5. New Moor Allerton, Leeds, England (27 holes).

In late summer we began plans to return to Florida. We had become close friends with Audrey and Lee Geddes, Colin's sister in-law and niece. Sally and the kids planned to travel back by ship to Fort Lauderdale, and I would remain to finish projects. While talking this over, Sally and Lee agreed on a plan to include Lee in the trip back to Florida. This was a great idea and worked out nicely. As for me, I had some ideas of leaving the company but nothing firmly planned.

Larry McClure, a land developer from Atlanta, had traveled to Switzerland to visit with Sally and me in Geneva. He had asked me to design nine more holes for him at the Berkley Hills Golf Club in Atlanta, Georgia. In addition, Gary Player had expressed interest in partnering with me to design projects he was learning about. This gave me a lot to think about.

As it happened, my return to Florida was received very coolly from Rees Jones, Robert's son in Montclair, New Jersey. Sadly, I told Mr. and Mrs. Jones I was leaving the company immediately. Mr. Jones had been a great influence on our lives, and Sally and I were sorry to have my job with Mr. Jones end, but we were hopeful for the future. I will always be thankful for the opportunities he gave me, and the experience to work with such a master. Our next stop was in Georgia.

Group at the Open Championship in St. Andrews, Scotland

Group at the Open Championship in Troon, Scotland

Group at the Open Championship in St. George's, England

LITTLE JOHN DR
LILBURN, GA

9th Hole

Little John Drive

Atlanta, Georgia

1970-1986

We sold our house in Plantation, Florida and moved into Larry McClure's house at Berkley Hills Golf Club in Atlanta. Larry was living in Clayton, Georgia, building a ski and golf resort named Sky Valley. My arrangement with Larry was to trade the design for a nine-hole extension of the existing eighteen holes at Berkley

Hills for the use of his and his wife, Sandra's, house on the golf course. We had purchased a new home under construction on Little John Drive in Lilburn, but it would be a few months before we could move in.

Living and working from Larry's house was a nice way to get us acclimated to the Atlanta area. We were active members at Berkley Hills Golf Club and very soon became members of the new Atlanta Athletic Club in Duluth, Georgia. Getting schools organized for Faye and Ron Jr. worked out well. Faye attended Duluth High School, and Ron Jr. enrolled at the Marist School in Atlanta. Beverly became a proper kindergartener at Town and Country in Lilburn. Lee continued to help Sally and me with all the relocation details and issues we faced during this period. Eventually, Lee moved to Clayton, Georgia to work in sales at the front office of Larry's Sky Valley Resort. She worked for Larry another ten years before moving back to England, marrying a baker named Eric Bell, and eventually retiring to Southern Spain in a grand villa above Mijas.

Soon after arriving in the Atlanta area, Ray Jensen, the owner of the Southern Turf Nurseries, called me to discuss a future meeting to possibly join forces with Arthur Davis, a graduate of the University of Georgia, working alone as a golf course architect. Arthur and I met in his office in Atlanta and realized we could help each other. The prospect of having Gary Player as our PGA Tour player partner was discussed, and we agreed this would be the ideal arrangement for our budding firm.

Arthur had one eighteen-hole design contract at Lake Lanier Islands, and I had the Berkley Hills nine-hole extension and some minor renovation jobs ongoing. Later in 1970, after a meeting with Gary and his IMG Management group, Davis, Kirby, and Player Golf Course Designers became a reality. Arthur produced the drawings and specifications from the office; I developed clients and supervised construction. Gary promoted our team. We had success locally and captured assignments internationally. Two years later, Arthur left the team to continue as a golf architect, and Gary and I stayed active for another five years (Kirby, Player, and Associates) before the firm became Kirby, Griffiths, and Associates. Denis Griffiths had been the first designer we hired in 1970. The word "partner" best describes our relationship, and I am proud to continue calling Denis my partner today.

Maintaining an office in Atlanta was a challenge; our first location was northwest of the city at Dunwoody Park off Interstate 285. We then moved to Peachtree Corners in Norcross and later built our own office building off Beaver Ruin Road by rezoning and converting a single-family home into a neat golf design office with our own short putting course. This became the home of the "Greater Norcross Open," an annual party for our friends and colleagues using one club and a whiffle golf ball. Another annual event that added to the social highlights was the "Singleton Clam Bake Lobster Party," in which John Singleton, a fellow North Shore of Boston native and sales representative for the Toro Company, would ship live lobsters and clams from Massachusetts down to Georgia for a night of fun with friends.

Living in our new house in Lilburn and traveling to southeast U.S. projects by car gave Sally and me a nice chance to visit Gatlinburg, TN, Savanah, GA, Hilton Head, SC, and even Palm Beach, FL. I thrived, thanks to the friendship and love that Sally brought into my relationships with all our owners. These friendships became especially strong and important with the many international owners and friends we had. Just to name a few of our invaluable relationships around the world, there was Hiroto San and family in Japan, Mike and Menchu Romero in the Philippines, Mark and Geraldine Muller and Robbie and Marie Marshal in South Africa, Paolo and Elisa Gueltrini and Antonio Stignani in Italy, Francisco and Carmen Lopez Segales in Spain, Alister Smith and family in Scotland, and, last but not least, Colin and Pauline Geddes in England. Travel to these international projects added so much excitement to our lives. Locally, we became friends with Tim and Jan Mcfall through Gary Player. Tim and I played many rounds of golf at the Atlanta Athletic Club and overseas. Later, Tim was kind enough to write a personal letter to Jack Nicklaus in support of my joining Golden Bear Golf Design in 1986.

Golf memberships were always part of our lifestyle. Our Berkley Hills membership was followed by years as members of the Atlanta Athletic Club, full of memories of dear friends and good golf games. Sally had a hole-in-one twice at No. 11 on the Riverside course in consecutive years. Sally met Kay Smith at the Atlanta Athletic Club, and they became golfing partners for life. We had a lot of fun playing with Kay and her husband, Tom ("Teeter"), in couples' golf days. Just one invitation to the British Open Championship led to many more annual British Open trips with Kay, Tom, and their family.

Sally did not just play golf. She later found success in real estate. It was interesting how this opportunity fell into her lap. She had stopped to look at a development of new condominiums on the way home from the Athletic Club. Soon after, she brought me to have a look at the model unit. After a tour of the model and talks with the owner, Paul Barrow, who was also a friend from Sea Pines on Hilton Head Island, Paul asked her if she wanted a job selling the units. Paul was impressed with Sally and said she was a natural at meeting and greeting prospective buyers. She loved showcasing new housing developments for Paul. Later in life, Sally found one for us as well as for other Athletic Club members.

Our staff at Kirby, Griffiths, and Associates included our office administrative assistant, Beverly Bilek, upstairs at the front desk, and Rodney Wright in plan development downstairs. Numerous others, mostly interning from the University of Georgia, came through the office over the years: Harrison Minschew, Clyde Johnston, Randy Russell, and Pat Joiner to name a few. Tom Johnson joined for field work in Asia and later became a solid part of Denis's team. We had a very relaxed working environment. We felt that if people were relaxed and enjoyed where they worked, they would be more creative. Moreover, it made for a lot of fun in those days.

Two international projects need to be mentioned here because of the timing and challenges. First, the Sun City Golf Course in Bophuthatswana, South Africa. In February of 1977, the hotel developer, Sol Kirshner, arranged for Gary Player and me to fly by helicopter from Johannesburg west to a barren, dry, desert-like site where he was constructing a major hotel and casino development. He said he wanted to have a championship eighteen-hole golf course worthy of hosting a major golf tournament, constructed here. The location was questionable, but water was promised from the Elands River and a large lake was planned for water storage and water sports.

After ten months of fast-track construction and travel, the first $1 million tournament in the world took place that December featuring the top ten professionals in the world. Forty years later that golf course looks and plays fantastic.

The second course of which I would like to detail the development is the Lake Poway Golf Course at Laoag in the Northern Philippines. In 1978, while I was on a construction site visit in North Carolina, the office in Atlanta called the pro shop to inform me that I had a call from the Philippines and to be ready to receive a call within minutes from Mrs. Imelda Marcos, the wife of the president of the Philippines. Within minutes I was indeed speaking to Mrs. Marcos, whom we had met on previous trips to the Philippines. Our conversation went something like this:

Mrs. Marcos: *The President turns sixty in September this year.*

Ron: *Very nice.*

Mrs. Marcos: *We want to build him a golf course in his home town of Laoag.*

Ron: *Very nice.*

Mrs. Marcos: *Can you build eighteen holes by September?*

Ron: *No, it's June now.*

Mrs. Marcos: *Can you build nine holes by September?*

Ron: *No, it's not possible.*

Mrs. Marcos: *Can you build one hole by September?*

Ron: *Yes.*

Mrs. Marcos: *Great! We will get nine contractors to each build one hole. When can you start?*

For his birthday in September, President Marcos played nine holes at the Poway Course in Laoag.

The Atlanta office was established in early 1970, and after sixteen years of golf course design projects in the United States and overseas, we were recognized as an international golf design company. Denis and I were asked to join the American Society of Golf Course Architects, and we were voted in at the meeting in Palm Springs in 1985. This was a proud achievement for both of us. In later years, Rodney Wright, Randy Russell, Clyde Johnston, and Tom Johnson, all alumni from our office, also became members. In attending annual meetings, Sally and I developed long lasting friendships with fellow members and their wives. It has been an honor to be part of this distinguished group of golf designers. Paul Fulmer was a dedicated director and leader of this association for many years, and now Chad Ritterbusch is carrying on those duties most competently. I was awarded fellow status in 2003.

In late 1986, I had an opportunity to use my international expertise and move forward in my career path. The Nicklaus design team was growing, and Jack's company was signing great projects both in the U.S. and overseas. Gene Bates, Faye's husband, had worked with us on construction in South Africa and the Philippines and was now working with the Nicklaus group. During a site visit with Jack, the need for a full-time designer living in Europe was discussed. Gene offered my name, and Jack agreed that I would be a perfect fit. And that is how the next big break evolved for Sally and me. A move back to Europe was in our immediate future.

Imelda Marcos on site visith with the President and Ron

Kirby Griffths and Associates design team –
Denis and Linda Griffiths, and Rodney Wright

Ron, Sally, Bud and Vi at Pebble Beach for the ASGCA Meeting

Ron and Sally with Gary and Vivienne Player,
and Jack and Barbara Nicklaus

Lawn party at Moor Allerton Golf Club in Yorkshire, England

Carlos Ochoa, John Singleton, Gary Player, Ron
and Miguel Romero – Wak Wak Golf Club

Sally, Faye, Ron Jr., Bev and Ron celebrating
Sally's 60th Birthday in Nassau

Our dear friends Kay and Tom (Teeter) Smith

Pauline and Janine Geddes with Sally and
Faye enjoying tea at the Ritz in London

Part Two

THE BACK NINE

FONTVIEILLE
DONATELLO HOUSE
MONACO

10th Hole

DONATELLO HOUSE

MONACO

1986-1989

The transition from my own design company with Denis to becoming a Senior Designer for the Golden Bear was a huge step. It meant relocating from Atlanta and establishing a residence in Europe. Leaving the team with Denis at the helm was sad, but the opportunity was so outstanding and natural, it had to happen. It was agreed that some preliminary design assignments such as cost estimates or feasibility studies would be directed to Denis's group in Atlanta along with one set of construction drawings for Collingtree, a new course located in Northhampton, England.

Deciding where we should reside took some travel and research, checking on permits. A railroad pass was helpful in our search for the right place. Our friend Carlos Ochua from the Toro Company helped by showing us the area in and around Monaco. One of our clients from Milan had news of an apartment available for rent in the Fontvielle neighborhood in Monaco. We were thus able to get settled at the Donatello House in Fontvielle, a new development with a lot of new construction. This location was nothing short of what anyone would imagine living on the French Riviera. Many scenic yacht harbors, beaches, restaurants, and sidewalk cafes. It was close to the heliport by the Princess Grace Rose Garden. That was good for connecting to flights to and from the Nice airport.

David and Joan Sherman, Nicklaus's company lawyer and his wife, arrived in Monaco from Palm Beach to set up a proper office. Once the office was established, a French design assistant, Francois Bouchard, was hired. We had a small apartment for design work, and David had a nice conference room and an executive assistant. Later, Dave Heatwall, a young architect from Palm Beach, came to Monaco to join our design team. Early travel led us to a second course at La Moraleja in Madrid, the Gut Altentann course in Salzburg, Austria, a new course at La Robinie in Milan, the Collingtree

Project in England, Gleneagles in Scotland, and Mount Juliet in Ireland. Later travel took us to numerous projects that had developed in Paris, London, and southern Spain. Clearly this chance to work with Jack Nicklaus was like attending a finishing school in golf design.

Sally made friends as usual, with both local and fellow Americans living in Monte Carlo. We enjoyed having friends and family visit and traveling by car to experience the wonders of the south of France and Italy. For a while we rented a BMW 700 Series, but eventually Sally found a Honda Civic wagon that worked out great. In fact, we ended up shipping that car to England when we moved there. Grand Prix Race Week is a special time in Monte Carlo. It's noisy as hell and wild with a lot of colorful events. One year we had friends from Spain visit, and in 1988 our daughter Beverly and her new husband John visited as part of their honeymoon. Ultimately, Sally would leave town during Race Week because it was so noisy and crowded. I ended up staying in town and watching for a couple of more years.

Living in Fontvielle by the port and stadium had its challenges. It is far down the huge hillside from the main area of Monte Carlo; luckily, we figured out bus service and utilized the town's elevators. The general way to get anywhere in Monte Carlo is to use an elevator that gets you up and down throughout the town. This must have had something to do with Grace Kelly's family being contractors. We found it easier to drive to

Nice to do our grocery shopping in large grocery stores where we stocked up on items we needed.

We played golf in Monaco at a course called Mount Gel, located in the mountains above Monte Carlo. This is where we watched a few Monte Carlo Open golf tournaments. Golf development was not very active in this area because the land is too valuable. However, we did secure a couple of design projects—one for Sean Connery on a property close to Cannes. We proposed layouts and options and had a site visit with Jack and Sean; this project was delayed and later sold. Another project was a "Cayman Ball" course design close to Nice, which unfortunately did not get off the ground but did get some design efforts. Work in other parts of Europe was active. Ultimately, plans to relocate our office to London began, and the adventure in Monaco came to an end. We were happy to get back on the wrong side of the road.

Ron and his mom Ethel (Mimi) in Monaco

Jack Nicklaus and Ron – Finishing School of Golf Design

Dave Heatwall, Jack Nicklaus and Ron at work

Maltman's Lane
Gerrards Cross

11th Hole

Maltman's Lane

(Note: Remember to drive on the left)

Gerrard's Cross, London England

1989-1992

T he relocation from Monaco, which provided a rough office set up, to the first-class office complex in the Chelsea area of London was outstanding. Our team had really grown and occupied three floors. David Sherman and his secretary were on the first floor with a nice conference room; on the second floor were David's assistant, Clemmons Goess Strauss, as well as John Copeland and Jay Sporl, who headed up maintenance and new construction. The designers, Dave Heatwall, Russell Talley, Francois Bouchard, Dirk Bouts, and myself, were on the third floor,

The Kings Road area along the River Thames had all one could ask for regarding convenience and support, very different from our neighborhood in Monaco. In addition to our comfortable office, golf was available to us at the Wentworth Golf Club, which had three courses. Being able to play at such fine courses was a real treat. Sally and I enjoyed playing the older and shorter courses.

The office move was well organized, and the timing perfect because we were at the end of our lease for the Donatello house in Fontvielle. Members of the team had different needs and requests for living arrangements—some wanted in-town apartments; others wanted to live outside town. Sally somehow found Maltman's Lane in the town of Gerrard's Cross; it was the perfect house in the most perfect, small English town fifteen miles outside London. Maltman's Lane was quaint with fine older estate homes and a private school.

The house next to us, Silver Birch, was owned by a woman named Peggy Miles and her husband, Austin, who was retired from the Royal Air Force. As expected,

Sally and Peggy became dearest friends. Peggy is Welsh and speaks perfect English. Across the street were the Davies, another really kind and friendly family that became close friends. Luckily, we saw Colin and Pauline often when they visited their daughter Janine who lived nearby. Colin took the head greenskeeper position at the new Handbury Manor Golf Club, which we were building near Cambridge. Our social life was active; this, along with the great British TV and sports, made our life in England wonderful. We even brought my dad, PK, over for a long vacation one summer, and he loved it.

The project list for Nicklaus Golf Design grew each year. We got more and more interesting sites for the firm. One major project was at London Golf in the town of Seven Oaks, south of London. London Golf is thirty-six holes on a large rolling hillside. The Japanese owner decided to have one Jack Nicklaus signature course and one Golden Bear course with a Ron Kirby Design.

Nicklaus's course opened with Jack playing Tony Jacklin and Seve Ballesteros. My course held a Senior European Tour event, won by John Bland, a friend of Jack's and mine. Our owner from Mt. Juliet, Tim Mahoney, was at the opening of Jack's course. Mount Juliet has held the Irish Open three years running and planned to hold it in May of 2020; however, due to The Republic of Ireland's strict Covid-19 quarantine measures, the decision was made to move it to Galgorm

Estate in Northern Ireland. The Gleneagles Nicklaus course went on to host the Scottish Open and recently the Ryder Cup. I am very proud of all who worked on this project to make it such a success.

La Moraleja II Golf Course in Madrid matured nicely with Francisco and Anthony as the head greenskeepers. It hosted the World Cup that Davis Love and Fred Couples won for the U.S.A. La Moraleja II remains an outstanding course in the Madrid region. Our work in Paris was exciting. We developed a signature course, Paris International, and Urban Cely, a Golden Bear design.

Upon turning sixty in 1992, I decided to retire from my fulltime assignment with Golden Bear in Europe yet continue to work as needed on a part-time basis stateside. Rather than fly back to the U.S., we decided to take a transatlantic voyage home in December of 1992. We invited Vi and Bud to fly to London and sail back to America with us on a Princess cruise ship. It was on this voyage that I signed up for watercolor lessons. The instructor, a classic Welsh woman, told Sally to buy me a paint set for Christmas and encourage me to paint. That was the beginning of my watercolor hobby, which led to the annual printing of calendars featuring my paintings, sent to friends and family at Christmas.

Sally had reserved a property with Paul Barrow at the new Spinnakers development on Lake Windward in Alpharetta, Georgia. Now it was time to return to the U.S. and restart our American lifestyle.

SPINAKERS
ALPHARETTA GA

12th Hole

SPINNAKERS – LAKE WINDWARD

ALPHARETTA, GEORGIA

1992 – 1998

O ur life back in the States following our European adventures in Monaco and England began at a new lakefront home in the Spinnakers development on Lake Windward in Alpharetta, Georgia, thirty miles north of Atlanta. Sally's association with Paul Barrow, the developer, had allowed us the ability to reserve the best lot in this new neighborhood. Sally was able to make a few trips to Atlanta during the construction phase to help make this our dream home featuring a boat dock and small sailboat that we named the "Sally Ann."

The house was terrific, the location perfect. Sally kept busy furnishing the house; we even adopted a kitten named Kudzu whom we spoiled rotten. Vi and Bud decided to move from California to a nice home also in the Lake Windward community which happened to be right around the corner from Kay and Tom (Teeter) Smith. Bud bought a pontoon boat and kept it at our dock. Many evenings were spent on that pontoon cruising around the lake at cocktail time. Better still, we had kept our golf membership at the Atlanta Athletic Club, so we were able to resume our regular golf games with friends.

My father, PK, joined us at the Spinnakers, buying the last model available when the development sold out. This worked out great as we could care for him in his old age. In fact, as my mother, Ethel, aged, it seemed she and PK grew closer, having many common interests. You see PK's wife, Alice, had passed away from cancer, and he was pretty lonely. There was a time when Sally thought we should move Ethel from Hollywood, Florida to Alpharetta, Georgia to live with PK, and maybe they could rekindle their love in their old age. That did not happen, but it was fun to think about. PK spent his time watching golf on TV and visiting with Scott Womack, the golf professional at the Pro Golf Discount store. John Singleton was a frequent visitor to the Spinnakers and hosted many lobster cookouts at our dockside.

As we attempted to settle into retirement, we soon realized there was no slowing down for me. I had made an arrangement with Nicklaus's Golden Bear Company upon my departure to be available to help as needed with projects I had been involved with for about seventy-five days per year. This arrangement eventually phased out as those projects reached completion. But then a new project for Nicklaus developed in Knysna, South Africa, on the south coast from one of my prior connections. Thus, it was agreed that I would continue as a liaison for the Simola Golf Club. Sally and I enjoyed a few trips back to South Africa to check on this project and visit with friends. A couple of other projects also fell into place at this time. One was a redesign of eighteen holes at Fort McPherson Army base in Atlanta that took a couple of seasons, closing nine holes each year. The other came from Randy Worls, the general manager at Oglebay Park in Wheeling, West Virginia, who contacted me to design a third eighteen-hole course. It was apparent my future consulting career was beginning to take form and would become the next phase in Sally's and my lives.

The growth of golf in Europe was on the rise in most countries, including Germany and Italy. As it related to me, I was asked to help set up a golf design team for Golf Invest, an Italian development company that was investing in golf real estate projects. We were busy chasing leads throughout Italy, including Tuscany and Pescara, as well as in Spain and Germany. I also assisted a German golf writer, Fritz Beindorf, with an eighteen-hole course in Krefeld, Germany. With all this new business and Golf Invest opening an office in Bergamo, Italy, there became a need for Sally and me to return to Europe to keep up with the work. We kept our Spinnaker house as our main residence, but spent most summers working overseas where we rented apartments in both Bergamo and Ravenna, Italy.

During this time, Sally and I made a trip to Mt. Juliet to attend the 1994 Irish Open. We had become close friends with owner Tim Mahoney, who in turn had introduced us to the Carr family. Roddy Carr had been involved in the project at Mt. Juliet from the start. Roddy Carr's dad, Joe Carr, was the Honorary Captain at Mt. Juliet. Joe was a famous amateur golfer and well known throughout Ireland. At one time, Joe Carr was captain of the R and A, and I like to refer to him as the "Arnold Palmer" of Ireland. At this Irish Open, Roddy told me his dad had been asked to design a new course in southwest Ireland at the Old Head site in Kinsale. He invited me to visit this extraordinary venue with them and to meet the owner, John O'Connor, and contractor, Haulie O'Shea. Upon that first visit to this take-your-breath-away site in Kinsale, and every time since, the view coming over the hill to the entrance is a "Wow" moment for me. It is truly a spectacular setting, perfect for a golf course that would become world-renowned.

Joe Carr had initially enlisted Paddy Merigan from the Sutton Golf Club to work with Haulie on the project. However, the chemistry among Paddy, Haulie, and owner John O'Connor turned tense, and later that year Paddy resigned. I was honored to be asked to take over the design assignment. Prior to that, my role with the Old Head team had been to develop green complexes that would best work for such an exposed and windy place. I had been visiting the site monthly and producing green sketches for a playable strategy plus re-routing to create more cliffside holes. In this ever-expansive role as lead designer, Sally and I needed to position ourselves in Kinsale, Ireland.

The first few summers we rented temporary accommodations at Ballinacurra House in Ballinspittle and an apartment in Kinsale. We then occupied a long-time rental at the Ardbrack development for about five years. The Old Head Golf Club opened for play in 1998, and the clubhouse opened in 2000 with Jim O'Brien as general manager. During these Kinsale years, Sally enjoyed assisting Ann O'Brien, Jim's wife, in the pro shop. Jim and Ann became our dear friends. My assignment at Old Head has never ended. Yearly improvements are regularly applied for this magnificent golf course.

This period of our lives unexpectedly became busy, splitting our time among the U.S., Ireland, and Italy. We wouldn't have wanted it any other way. I was doing what I loved to do, and Sally was making many friends and memories along the way.

We made over 12 Transatlantic Cruise Crossings

Old Head #6 Green

Ron finishing #17 green at Old Head

Ron and Patrick O'Connor at Old Head

Ron and Roddy Carr at Old Head

Sally and Ann O'Brien at Old Head Pro Shop

Ron and Paolo Gueltrini in Pescara, Italy

Old Head Golf Links #4.
Voted into the Best 18 holes of golf .... in the world

Old Head Golf Links.
View from the Clubhouse

BERGAMO ALTO
ITALY

13th Hole

BERGAMO, ITALY

1993-1994

Projects in Italy were gaining popularity as golf became more exposed at golf tournaments and scenic resort areas. The newly formed company of Golf Invest, a division of the parent company Fin Invest, established an office in Bergamo, Italy.

Sally and I visited Bergamo to look for a place to live in this quaint old Italian city. Bergamo has two towns: Bergamo Alta is at the top of the hill, beautiful and scenic. Downtown Bergamo is where the Golf Invest offices were located. Halfway up the hill, we found a nice apartment, which was both scenic as well as convenient for Sally to do her shopping and me to do my work.

Bergamo is close to Lake Como, Milan, and Venice. It was no surprise that we had many friends from all over the world come to visit us. Our favorite place was Bellagio on Lake Como. We also spent many weekends in Venice. Visitors included our daughter Beverly and her friend Jeanine, Kay and Tom (Teeter) Smith and family from Atlanta, Peggy Miles from Maltman's Lane, Mark Muller, and our new friend, Ola Grinnaker, from the Knysna project in South Africa. Sally had a knack for making everyone feel welcome.

My assignment at Golf Invest was exciting. In developing the team, I was introduced to Paolo Gueltrini and Anthony Stignani, landscape architects with an office in Ravenna, Italy. Paolo and I traveled all over the Italian countryside in an Alfa Romeo sedan equipped with a car phone investigating housing and proposing golf projects. Naples, Bologna, Modena, Rome, Florence, and San Tropez are a few of the cities we explored.

Unfortunately, local town elections made the permit process difficult for gaining project approval. After two years, Golf Invest closed; we moved out of the apartment in Bergamo and stayed a few months in Ravenna to help Paolo and Antonio complete the projects in Pescara and Modena.

We rented a small apartment in Ravenna. Sally got a bicycle and enjoyed going to the local market to shop each morning for groceries and became close friends with Paolo's wife, Lisa. She loved all the shops in Ravenna and made friends with many owners. The famous sweater purchase was heart stopping for Sally. Asking at the time how much anything costs in Italy was a nightmare as the lira and dollar exchange could have been about sixty thousand to one. When Sally bought a beautiful, mixed color sweater, she thought she paid about eighty U.S. dollars. Later, I had to tell her it was over eight hundred U.S. dollars! After a failed attempt for a refund, this sweater became infamous. I always told her she looked like a million lira when she wore it.

At this time, my primary focus became the ongoing project at Old Head; therefore, Sally and I found ourselves splitting time now between Georgia and Kinsale, Ireland.

The famous Italian sweater

SATIN ∧ LACE
KINSALE

14th Hole

SATIN AND LACE

(Note: Remember to drive on the left)

KINSALE, IRELAND

1998–1999

Our Spinnakers lakeside house in Georgia remained our main residence, but with on-going projects in design and construction in Ireland, on the Continent, and in the Canary Islands, travel to Europe became a normal spring and summer event. The apartment we rented in Kinsale was above a lingerie store called Satin and Lace. We found this location quaint and convenient to many shops and restaurants. We enjoyed our time in the town of Kinsale, frequenting Mother Hubbard's for a full Irish breakfast after stopping at Mozie's Favorites for the newspapers, as well as many dinners at Man Friday's, Jim Edwards, and the Blue Haven. Another frequent stop between Old Head and Kinsale was the Speckled Door Pub, owned by John and Magdalena Lourgan.

Old Head continued to mature and improve. Noel Hurley, who used to be the gatekeeper, became the caddymaster. Noel hired our grandson, David Bates, to join the caddy program, and he was able to caddy for two seasons.

Another way we traveled was by cruise ship at least in one direction. We found discounts on repositioning cruises between the Caribbean and Mediterranean. Sally's favorite was Windstar's flagship the Wind Surf, a five masted vessel carrying approximately three hundred passengers. We traveled transatlantic twice on the Wind Surf. We also sailed with Celebrity and Princess Cruise Lines. We even traveled by container ship one year. Upon returning to Atlanta every fall, we soon realized that the Georgia weather was cold and dreary, so we began to consider a move to South Florida.

A new opportunity arose on the west coast of Ireland in Waterville. The contractor for the Old Head golf course, Haulie O'Shea, owned land and a hotel in Waterville and asked me to design an eighteen-hole course. With very little budget, Haulie and I worked together over the next few years and built Skellig Bay. Jim O'Brien helped Haulie open and establish the course, and Ann O'Brien helped with the pro shop operation. Skellig Bay Golf Club was popular among local Irishmen and provided tourists an additional course to play in Waterville. In 2015, Haulie lost the course due to financial issues. It was re-done by Robert Trent Jones Jr. and later opened as Hogs Head Golf Club, named after the skyline of Skellig Bay.

One unfortunate event during this time that had a huge impact on Sally's life was a jaw problem caused by a bad dental procedure. Sally went in for some routine dental work, and the effects of the procedure caused her to suffer jaw discomfort for the rest of her life. Later, she was diagnosed with a muscle disorder called dystonia, in which the muscles contract and prevent the jaw from resting straight. She had trouble eating and talking, a big part of Sally's social life. She sought help all over the world, including the Mayo Clinic and Cleveland Clinic; she even saw experts in London on Harley Street. There was no cure, but she did find temporary relief with periodic Botox injections administered by a doctor at the University of Minnesota.

It was during this time in Kinsale that Sally went to Harley Street in London for help with her jaw problem. After meeting with a team of experts in the morning, she was on a lunch break when a courier on a motorbike ran her down. This was a hit and run accident leaving poor Sally in the street, injured badly, suffering from a broken pelvis and bruises all over her body. I was traveling in Spain and could not get to London until the next day. Luckily, Noreen Collins, our friend from Kinsale, boarded a flight from Cork to London and got to her immediately. Upon release from the hospital, we stayed at Patrick O'Connor's house in London until Sally was able to travel. It just so happened the British Open was taking place in St. Andrews the week after the accident. Despite being on crutches, Sally insisted we drive to St. Andrews to be with friends who had traveled from the U.S. and England for our annual British Open festivities.

The return to Kinsale after the accident and British Open led us to find a more accessible place to live. The Satin and Lace apartment was on the third floor, and Sally was not able to climb stairs. Through friends, we found a new and nicely furnished house in the Ardbrack neighborhood of Kinsale, and we moved into this home and ultimately extended the lease for the next five years.

Sally on crutches after London knock down

ARD BRACK
KINSALE IRELAND

15th Hole

ARDBRACK

(Note: Remember to drive on the left)

KINSALE, IRELAND

1999-2005

This was a very active time for us. We were spending half the year at the Spinnakers and the other half at Ardbrack in Kinsale. Sally turned sixty, and the kids and I celebrated with a special trip down memory lane to Paradise Island in the Bahamas, where it all started. We had a nice reunion with our Nassau friends, Butch and

Anna Carey, who had worked at the Bahamas Country Club.

The stateside projects at Ft. McPherson in Atlanta and Oglebay Park in West Virginia were well underway. The new course design at Oglebay was awarded to the Arnold Palmer Design group, but my close friend and general manager of Oglebay, Randy Worls, was able to keep me involved by allowing me to be a liaison between the hired contractor for the job, Randy Vaughts, and the Palmer Group. Projects in Europe, Spain, and Ireland filled the summer months.

Additional projects in Ireland began to surface through my affiliation with the Carr Golf Group. A major housing development and golf project became active in Dublin at Killeen Castle. It became apparent that finding accommodations closer to Dublin would be best for Sally and me. Roddy Carr put me in touch with Brian and Carol Wallace in Dublin. Brian Wallace was part owner of the Killeen Castle golf project. He and Carol became our close friends, and they helped us find a place to live in Howth along the harbor in Dublin for a few summers. We enjoyed our time living seaside, and as usual, Sally made many friends among neighbors and shop keepers.

Dromoland Castle asked me to upgrade their eighteen-hole Castle Course hotel layout with the goal of having golf travelers stay and play at their course along with courses like Lahinch and Ballybunion. Paolo's office in Ravenna helped with the drawings needed for these new projects, and I continued to work with them on their jobs in Modena, Bologna, and Canary Islands.

I began working with the group called TurfGrass, founded by John Clarkin, an agronomist in the Dublin area, as many Irish courses used TurfGrass for their agronomy services. John Clarkin continues to be a big part of our life story and is considered part of the family.

Sally and I made a few trips during this time to South Africa to meet Ola Grinnaker, who was introduced to us by Mark Muller and Robbie Marshall, whom he had contacted in hopes of converting his farm in Knysna on the southern coast of South Africa into a golf course called Simola. Ola was a decorated military helicopter pilot and war hero who became disabled in combat and suffered a bad leg. He flew his own private helicopter every day at the farm, and on one of our visits flew Sally and me to the Cape Town airport for our flight home, stopping at pretty sites all along the Garden Route. Ola became a dear friend.

The Knysna property had outstanding vistas high above the coastline. However, this presented many construction challenges due to the steep grades and difficulties with irrigation. We brought Ola to Ireland and other projects in Europe to show how complex his project was. Later, Ola decided to engage the Nicklaus Design organization to help create and market the Simola project in Knysna. Sean Quinn, the design assistant working with Mark and Robbie in South Africa, got his start on this course and ended up joining the Nicklaus Company.

Sadly, on September 11, 2001 we all got the greatest shock when terrorists destroyed the twin towers in New York City, killing thousands. Everything was turned upside down, and travel has never been the same. Our journeys through airports became full of delays and challenges. Thus, Sally and I decided to rethink all of the travel we had been doing and realized we needed to get back to what we needed most, time at home with family and friends. Our next stop was to be near our daughter Faye, her husband Gene, and family in North Palm Beach, Florida in a high-rise apartment at Governor's Point. Some travel was still required to fulfill obligations with the current projects, but we committed ourselves to slowing down and looking forward to enjoying family again.

Robbie Marshall, Ron and Mark Mueller in South Africa

Ron and John Clarkin onsite at Stagsridge in Ireland

GOVERNORS POINT
NORTH PALM BEACH

16th Hole

GOVERNORS POINT

NORTH PALM BEACH, FLORIDA

2000-2002

We began to rethink spending the rainy, cold winters in Atlanta at the Spinnakers. Our daughter Faye, her husband, Gene, and two children, Denise and David, had been living in North Palm Beach since 1985. Sally and Faye got busy looking for homes and found the Governors Point apartments overlooking the North Palm Beach Country Club and intercoastal waterway.

It was a perfect location. We joined the North Palm Beach Country Club, and it became our center of activity. Members became our new friends, many of whom traveled to Ireland to visit us during the hot summer months. Sally and Faye played team golf for the North Palm Beach Ladies. Life was good in Florida, our plan being November to May in Florida and May through October in Ireland. The Irish projects were either in the process of design, construction, or maturing nicely.

Dominic Daly, a board member at the Old Head, had brokered a real estate deal in Castlemartyr, and gave my name to the developer as they were planning to build a resort hotel and an eighteen-hole golf course. I was awarded the job and worked with Matt Swanson and son-in-law Gene Bates on this project. I also used John Clarkin's team at TurfGrass to help with the scope of building an inland Ireland links type course rather than another parkland castle course. TurfGrass brought Trevor Norris into this project. Trevor grew in the course and presented the members and hotel guests with a unique links golf course. My concepts worked; some blind greens are tricky, but the course is a success. This project was an exciting challenge, and Sally and I rented a holiday seaside apartment in Ballycotton over two summers while it was completed.

The Killeen Castle course owner, Brian Wallace, advised he needed a marquee name for the major hotel to be involved, so we got the Jack Nicklaus group to take over, and I remained as liaison between Brian and Jack's teams, completing this project while living in the Dublin area. The course has a beautiful setting and makes for great television as it hosted the Solheim Cup in 2011. Unfortunately, the hotel never was built, and the golf course operates more like a local members' course rather than a resort.

We enjoyed living in Howth on the seafront. We were given golf privileges at Sutton Golf Club and played often on long summer nights. We had many great dinners in town with Dermot Gilleece, a famous golf writer in Ireland, and his wife, Kathy. Dermot's weekly column in the *Irish Independent* will always give me something to remember. Joe Carr passed away while we were living in Howth. Following the memorial service at the local church, Sally arranged a reception at our apartment for friends of Joe's and ours. Sally always made friends welcome.

My father, PK, had also passed away during this time. I was in Waterville at the Skellig Bay project working on the sixth hole when Haulie came out to tell me Sally had called with the news that PK had died. Haulie and I spent the next couple of hours reflecting on PK's life. Haulie named the sixth hole "Reflection" in honor of the day.

My overseas projects outside Ireland included the Canary Islands in Spain along with a new twenty-seven-hole project in Copenhagen, Denmark called Royal Golf Club. Gene's group in Florida produced construction plans and specifications again, and Casey Bates, Gene's nephew, was hired by the owner to shape all the features.

Sally joined me on a few trips to Denmark as it gave us a chance to visit with our friend Ian Tomlinson, the superintendent at Rungsted Golf Club in Denmark, and his wife, Linda, and their two boys. We also combined another site visit to Denmark with a Baltic cruise on Holland America, during which we visited St. Petersburg, Russia.

As for projects in the U.S., the new course for Oglebay Park was being constructed. I was acting as liaison among the general manager, Randy Worls, Randy Vaught's construction company, and Harrison Minschew, the design associate from the Palmer Group. This arrangement worked out nicely. The course was completed after a couple of seasons, and Randy Worls and his wife, Betty, visited us in Ireland one summer.

We soon realized apartment living at Governors Point was not the best place for us long term. We did not like having to use an elevator to get up and down to our beautiful living area. Sally, by happenstance, met a lady in the elevator who was looking for a two-bedroom apartment because she had decided to sell her three-bedroom home at Oaks East in North Palm Beach. The two exchanged numbers, and Sally visited the lady's home. It was indeed a three-bedroom home with a small pool and two-car garage in a gated community.

This was a perfect Florida house, and we decided to move from Governors Point to Oaks East later in 2002. I am still there today, but it is important to share with you the short time we spent in New Hampshire.

Living in South Florida, it is imperative to get out of the hot and humid summers. We were lucky enough to find a beautiful place in New Hampshire called Tidewatch, where we spent a couple of special summers.

Sally and Ron at Castlemartyr

Castlemartyr Golf Resort, County Cork, Ireland

TIDEWATCH
PORTSMOUTH M.H.

17th Hole

TIDEWATCH

PORTSMOUTH, NEW HAMPSHIRE

2005-2007

The Tidewatch venture for Sally and me began when we initially moved to North Palm Beach from Atlanta. Upon joining the North Palm Beach Country Club, we met many members, most of whom would leave Florida during the summer months for homes up north. Sally's dear friend Ann Lermer, with whom she played a lot of golf, had a place in Portsmouth, New Hampshire. On one of our trips back to Ireland, we stopped in to visit Ann in the Tidewatch development in Portsmouth, a very scenic town, where she had a lovely home.

Later that summer, Ann called Sally in Ireland and mentioned she was selling the house in Tidewatch and moving a short distance to another condominium development. Sally and I gave it some thought and decided this would be a good place for a second home. It would allow us to get out of Florida during the hot summers, and we would be able to have family and friends visit us. We called Ann back and told her we wanted to buy her house.

In the spring of 2005, we packed a few of our extra things into our SUV and drove to Portsmouth, New Hampshire. Sally enjoyed furnishing the entire house from various local consignment shops.

We loved having friends and family visit. Sally's sister June and her husband, George, who lived not far away in our hometown of Beverly, Massachusetts visited, as well as some of Sally's friends, including Mary Normand, a high school classmate from Beverly High School. Our daughter Beverly and her two young children came for a visit too.

Traveling to Ireland was an easy flight from Boston's Logan Airport when I needed to check on projects in the Emerald Isle. I got plenty of chances to paint my watercolors in and around beautiful Portsmouth. I painted the B.J. Boathouse as well as the famous tugboats in the harbor where we enjoyed many seafood dinners, including Sally's favorite, fried clams.

Our time in Tidewatch was short because we soon realized we did not want to own property in New Hampshire, especially in the winter, and sadly, Sally's sister June passed away in 2006. In addition, my projects in Ireland required us to be there during the summers, so after less than two years, we sold Tidewatch.

Sally and Ron with her sister June and
husband George at Tidewatch

ORKS EAST
PALM BEACH GARDENS

18th Hole

Oaks East

Palm Beach Gardens, Florida

2002-2020

This chapter of our story is the longest. It will tell how Sally and I finish this tale of two Beverly kids who have really done a lot. In looking back, it feels as though we spent half our lives on the wrong side of the road. The years we spent in Europe were some of the best memories we have. The dear friends we have made in this lifetime were like family to us.

The final move that we made to Oaks East was perfect timing. Eighteen years later, I am still enjoying the house. To best summarize our years here at Oaks East, I will focus on four main topics: family, health, travels, and design projects.

Faye graduated from Duluth High School in Duluth, Georgia and after two years at the University of Georgia went to work for Delta Airlines as a flight attendant in 1973. After thirty-eight years flying the friendly skies, Faye retired and enjoys playing a lot of golf. Faye and her husband, Gene, still live on the seventeenth hole at North Palm Beach Country Club. Gene stays active with golf design mostly in the western U.S. He became a member of the Association of Golf Course Architects in 2016. Faye and Gene have two children: a daughter Denise, who with husband Matt Kuntz and daughter Kendall live in Jupiter, Florida, and a son, David who lives in Massachusetts and has a daughter named Amelia. Denise is an avid equestrian with two horses that keep her busy. Matt plays golf at Tequesta Country Club where he is a board member and fine player. I spend a lot of time these days with Kendall, watching her ride horses, take tennis lessons, and swim. Recently, I have been teaching her art lessons and she is becoming quite the painter.

Ron Jr., following somewhat in the old man's footsteps, graduated turf school in Lake City, Florida, had a tour of duty for four years with the U.S. Navy, then returned to golf course work overseas. Later in life, he found a passion for driving big rigs, eighteen-wheelers, across the country; he will soon retire from that successful career and looks forward to golfing and windsurfing. Ron Jr. and wife, Oy, currently live in Brunswick, Georgia. Oy has a nice position working at a resort in Sea Island, Georgia. They both play golf and plan to play more in retirement. Their daughter, Sarah, lives in Austin, Texas and recently had a baby boy named Jaxon. Ron Jr. also has a daughter from a previous marriage, Marianne, who is an accomplished writer living in Washington, D.C. with her husband, Ed.

Beverly graduated from St. Pius X Catholic High School in Atlanta and later finished her degree at the University of Pittsburgh. She spent more than thirty years in the travel industry specializing in golf travel and event management. Beverly and her husband, John, recently moved to Riverside, California after twenty-five years in Minnesota. John leads The Toro Company's irrigation division, and both are active members at the Victoria Golf Club. They have two children: a son, Kirby, and daughter, Holly, who are both recent graduates from Miami University in Oxford, Ohio and are currently working at accounting firms in Minneapolis.

I have had heart issues most of my life, beginning with a heart attack in 1978 caused by stress. Luckily, rest and diet sufficed with no surgery needed. In 1995

I had bypass surgery performed by Dr. Murphy at Saint Joseph's Hospital in Atlanta, Georgia. Dr. Crandall of West Palm Beach became our heart doctor when we moved to Governors Point. I had two more minor episodes when stents were implanted and a major event for an aortic aneurism in 2015. A couple of years later while at Castlemartyr Golf Resort in Ireland, I was rushed to the University Hospital in Cork and required a pacemaker. Dr. Jamie Gibson from Waterville performed the procedure. Interestingly enough, Jamie, as a teenager, got his start picking rocks for me during the construction of the Old Head. Needless to say, I felt very comfortable having Jamie perform the surgery on me. The Irish pacemaker is doing fine.

Other than the chronic jaw issue, Sally was very healthy most of her life. However, in early 2000, while we were on a site trip to the Netherlands visiting Bram de Vos, the owner of the Oostburg Golf Club, Sally woke up feeling pins and needles in her left leg. She knew something was wrong as soon as we got back to Ireland later that evening. She saw Brian Wallace's doctor immediately, and he ordered an MRI, which confirmed a stroke. The MRI detected a small spot in the center of her brain, which had affected her left leg and would require a prescription of Lyrica the rest of her life. Another stroke occurred during our cruise aboard the *Equinox* in 2013 off the coast of Norway. This stroke was more serious and involved aphasia since it resulted in her loss of speech. Faye flew over to Bergen, Norway immediately and met us at the University Hospital. A week later, we all flew back to Florida where Sally began speech therapy twice a week. After six months of therapy, her speech was close to normal, but the jaw issue from the dental procedure years ago was still a major problem. Everything considered, until the last six months of 2019, Sally was in good form and able to enjoy a fairly active life for a very attractive woman of eighty-six years!

Sally and I realized late in life that while we had traveled the world to various golf projects, we had missed a lot of tourist sites that our friends had seen and enjoyed. We decided to make an effort to see some of the tourist sites that were not golf related. Between 2010–2018, we were able to take a Danube River cruise with our close friends Jane and Judge Emery Newell; we passed through the Suez Canal on the *Queen Elizabeth II*; we visited Niagara Falls with our nephew, Brian Sexten, and his wife, Linda; and, most recently, cruised through the Panama Canal after a visit to California with Beverly, John, and family.

Sally's sister Vi and her husband, Bud, had split their time between their home in Atlanta and a beautiful high-rise condominium in Old Port Cove, in North Palm Beach Florida. In 2008, the house right next door to us in Oaks East went up for sale, and they bought it. For many years we enjoyed having Bud and Vi live near us. They were a bit older than Sally and me, and as they aged, we were able to look after them. They have both since passed, but their son, Brian, and his wife, Linda, now live in the house next door, splitting their time between Palm Beach Gardens, Florida and Cleveland, Ohio. It is now Linda and Brian who look after me. I am so appreciative of all of their help with Sally as she was going through her health troubles last year. I am grateful beyond words to continue our many happy hours on our patios and evening dinners with each other.

Late last year, Doctor Crandall told me Sally was failing. It took me a long time to come to grips with this, but ultimately, I knew. There had been signs: her speech after the latest stroke had come back, but in the past year or so she began having more trouble finding the right words to communicate. In addition to this, there seemed to be a constant battle between her heart and lungs, resulting in a couple of procedures on her heart in the fall of 2019. She was very tired of not feeling well. In January of 2020, she made her last trip to Minnesota for a Botox injection to help with her ongoing jaw problem. Upon returning from Minnesota, she fell ill and was admitted to the hospital for pneumonia. Unfortunately, she never got better and suffered a massive stroke to which there would be no recovery. This tale ends with Sally's passing on January 31, 2020 at the age of eighty-six, with our entire family able to be with her to say our last goodbyes and my commitment to writing this book detailing the adventures of our wonderful life together.

I am carrying on as best I can, keeping Sally's memory with me at all times. Closing a golf design career isn't easy; I just cannot stop that part of my life. It only takes a phone call to ask for help with a one-hole problem or a major design for my creative juices to get active. Lately, the following assignments are just that.

In San Lorenzo, at a mountain lodge near Cortina, Italy, Paolo and I converted a helipad to a putting green with six decks of artificial turf in a pasture next door for tees. The owner is now delighted to have an eighteen-hole course above the clouds. I call this my heavenly green. The owners, Stefano Barbini and his wife, Georgiana, loved Sally.

At the Capard House in Port Laoise, Ireland, John Clarkin from TurfGrass called about a project called Stags Ridge for a private owner's residence. We constructed ten greens and fifteen tees so the owner can play as many as fifty-four different holes. The TurfGrass team of Trevor Norris and Glen Deegan provided quality in every way.

At Apes Hill Golf Club on the island of Barbados, Roddy Carr called and asked for help bringing back in play a scenic and challenging eighteen-hole course. This is the project I am working on now as I complete this memoir with Matt Swanson, a golf course designer in North Palm Beach, Florida, providing me plan production and drawings to scale.

At the Old Head in Kinsale Ireland, I will continue to visit and offer Jim O'Brien and Neil Deasy any assistance in finding ways to improve this masterpiece. They are currently working from a ten-year improvement plan that I provided a few years ago.

This life that Sally and I have led has been nothing short of extraordinary and a blessing. I could not have accomplished anything without her by my side. I would not have wanted to spend half my life on the wrong side of the road with anyone other than my dear, sweet, beautiful Sally. And while I still have a lot of living to do, not to mention many crossword puzzles and jumbles to solve, I know that Sally and I will be together again someday, on one side of the road.

END

Florida Family

Bev, John, Kirby and
Holly with Ron in Dana
Point, California

Ron Jr., Oy and Sarah

Ron and Sally with David and
Great Grandaughter Amelia

Ron with Great Grandaughter
Kendall - painting lessons

Ron's girls - Faye, Sally and Bev

Our wonderful daughter Faye

Florida Family with Holly visiting from Minnesota

Linda and Brian Sexten
at Niagra Falls

Faye, Gene, John, and Bev
enjoying a round of golf

Sally with Sarah and Oy
at Sea Island Georgia

Sally, Faye, Gene and
Ron at Cypress Point for
Ron's 60th Birthday

Ron, Bev and Sally at "Bev's Wine Bar" in Minneapolis

Francisco and Carmen Segales visit to the USA

Great picture of great friends; Judge Emery Newell, Barbara Hill, Jane Newell, Jack Hill, Sally, Ron, and Colin Geddes

Jane Newell, Jane Bahouth, Sally and Bev at annual
St. Patricks Charity Golf Tournament

Sally and Helen
Lester in Ireland

Noelle and Sally in Kinsale

Sally and Ron visiting Noreen
and her dog, Sparkie

Jo Ann Muller and Sally
in Palm Beach Gardens

John Clarkin and Ron in Kinsale, Ireland

Ron and Sally with Jim and Ann O'Brien at Castlemartyr, Ireland

Ron and Sally with Trevor Norris at Castlemartyr, Ireland

The Heavenly Hole - San Lorenzo Lodge in the Italian Alps

Ron and Kirby at Dromoland Caslte Golf Course

Judge Emery and Jane Newell with Ron
and Sally on a Danube Cruise

John Picerne and Ron at Stagsridge

Kirby and John Picerne at Stagsridge

Ron's design office

Anthony Bennett and Ron in Ireland

Ron finishing #5 green at Apes Hill in Barbados

19th Hole

Ron's Hall of Fame

Owners

Tim Mahoney

Mt. Juliet Golf Club, Kilkenny Ireland

John Picerne

Stags Ridge Golf Club, Port Laoise, Ireland

John & Patrick O'Connor

Old Head Golf Club, Kinsale, Ireland

Brian Wallace

Killeen Castle Golf Club, Dunshaughlin, Ireland

General Managers

Jim O'Brien

Old Head Golf Club, Kinsale, Ireland

Jim Melody

Woodbrook Golf Club, Dublin, Ireland

Marco Leria Couderc

Club de Golf Escorpion, Valencia, Spain

Mark Nolan

Dromoland Castle Golf Club, Shannon, Ireland

Golf Directors

Donald O'Quinn

Harbour Town Golf Links, Sea Pines, South Carolina

Breffne McKenna

Castlemartyre Golf Resort, Middleton, Ireland

Golf Superintendents

Every superintendent who grew
in and matured our courses

Restaurants

Chinese

The Ambassador, Cork, Ireland

Steak

Casa Paca, Plaza Mayor, Madrid, Spain

Fish

Joe's Stone Crab, Miami Beach, Florida

Italian

Ca' de Ven, Ravenna, Italy

Our favorite cruise experience ‑ "The Windsurf"

Acknowledgments

I would like to thank my longtime friend and favorite golf writer from Boston, Massachusetts, Gary Larrabee, who continued to encourage Sally and me over the years to get our life adventures down on paper so we could produce this memoir to share not only with family and friends, but anyone who may have an interest in golf. We have led a very full life blessed with numerous adventures and dear friends throughout the world.

Writing this memoir took many forms beginning with handwritten notes on yellow legal pads, audio recordings on mini-cassette tapes, and voice memos on my iPhone, which eventually found their way into a word document allowing us to move to the editing phase. I would not have been able to navigate this process without the help of my daughter, Beverly McPhee, who happened to retire during this time and was thus able to dedicate countless hours to this project. Beverly was able to gather my notes in all forms and creatively organize them, as well as edit each chapter.

They say it takes a village, and I am certainly grateful for my village of family and friends who took the time to read, re-read, edit, and offer insights into presenting the amazing life Sally and I shared. I also want to thank Lance Palmer and Mark O'Malley at the North Palm Beach Staples for their efforts scanning and positioning the many photos to help illustrate our incredible story.

Lastly, I would like to thank my dear sweet Sally for choosing me to share this life. Completing this project has given me a great sense of accomplishment knowing that our life of amazing adventures and friendships has been documented and communicated. I hope the readers of this book not only enjoy our tale, but also see what a thoughtful, caring, beautiful woman you were, Sally, and how honored I have been to have had you by my side for sixty-eight years.

Ron and Sally, two sweethearts - world travelers

RON KIRBY

Golf Course Designer

BACKGROUND

Elected fellow of the American Society of Golf Course Architects for his dedicated service to his profession and his outstanding contributions to the game of golf.

Member of the Massachusetts State High School Championship Golf Team 1949-50. Studied at the Boston Museum of Fine Arts in 1946-47. He then attended the University of Massachusetts Stockbridge School of Agriculture on a Francis Quimet Scholarship, receiving an Associate Degree in Agronomy in 1953.

Served as Superintendent on several golf courses, including one in the Bahamas designed by Dick Wilson. In the mid-1960s he was employed by Robert Trent Jones, Inc. building courses in the U.S. and England. In 1970 he formed an association with golf architect Arthur Davis based in Georgia. PGA professional Gary Player served for a time as a consulting partner in the firm. In the late seventies, Davis and Player left the firm, and associate Denis Griffiths became Kirby's partner. Joined Jack Nicklaus Golf Design services in 1986 and was responsible for all European projects.

Presently living in South Florida collaborating on design projects with the following teams and consultants:

- Stags Ridge Golf Course, County Laois, Ireland
- Kokkedal Golf Klub, Denmark
- Old Head Golf Links, Kinsale, Ireland
- Apes Hill Golf Club, Barbados
- John Clarkin, Turfgrass Consultancy, Dublin Ireland
- Bates Golf Design Group, Palm Beach Gardens, Florida
- Swanson Golf Design Company, Palm Beach Gardens, Florida

COURSES DESIGNED BY RON KIRBY

ALABAMA
CC of Alabama, Eufaula (1986)
North River GC, Tuscaloosa (1978)

COLORADO
Pole Creek GC, Tabernash (1983)

GEORGA
Alpine Valley, Berkley Hills GC, Norcross (1971)
Grimball GC, Savannah (1986)
Little Course, Norcross (1980)
Nob North GC, Dalton (1978)
Pebble Brook GC, Manchester (1970)
Pine Isle CC, Lake Lanier (1972)
River North G&CC, Macon (1973)
Royal Oaks GC, Cartersville (1971)

ILLINOIS
Holiday Inn CC, Crete (1970)

N. CAROLINA	Twin Valley CC, Wadesboro (1975)
S. CAROLINA	Dolphin Head GC, Hilton Head Island (1973)
	Marsh Point GC, Kiawah Island (1976)
TENNESSEE	Bent Creek Mountain Inn CC, Gatlinburg (1979)
TEXAS	Fair Oaks Ranch G&CC, Boerne (1979)
VIRGINIA	Brandermill CC, Midlothian (1976)
BARBADOS	Barbados GC (2000)
ENGLAND	London Golf Club, International Course 1990)
IRELAND	Old Head Golf Links, Kinsale Co. Cork (1999)
	Castlemartyr Resort GC, Castlemartyr, Co. Cork (2007)
	Skellig Bay, Waterville (2005)
ITALY	Pescara GC, Pescara Abruzzo (1995)
IVORY COAST	Riviera Africaine GC (1972)
JAPAN	Niigata Forest GC, Toyhoura Village (1975)
	Nishi Nihon GC, Nogata (1975)
	Odawara CC (1973)
	Sun Lake CC, Utsunomiya (1980)

PHILLIPINES   Kanirag GC, Cebu Island (1982)

Lake Paoay GC, Hocus Note (1979)

Peurto Azul GC, Pasay City (1980)

SOUTH AFRICA   Gary Player CC, Sun City (1979)

Roodepoort, (Municipal) (1985)

SPAIN   Almerimar GC, Almeria (1975)

El Pariso Esteponia (1972)

Maspalomas GC, North Course (1974)

Escorpian Golf Club, Valencia (1976)

COURSES REMODELED AND EXPANDED BY RON KIRBY

ALABAMA   Huntsville (Municipal) (1984)

FLORIDA   Everglades Club, Palm Beach (1984)

GEORGIA   Bacon Park CC, Savanah (1985)

Cartersville CC (1972)

Dalton CC, Atlanta (1973)

Ft. McPherson GC, Atlanta (1994)

Little Mountain CC (1970)

Sandy Run GC (1970)

Savannah GC (1989)

Standard Club, Atlanta (1971)

Warner Robins, AFB GC, Macon (1970)

LOUISIANA	New Orleans CC (1975)
MISSOURI	Bellerive CC, Creve Cooer (1985)
TEXAS	Fair Oaks Ranch G&CC, Boerne (1985) Hogan Park GC, Midland (1978) Oakhill CC, San Antonio (1978) Midland CC (1979)
VIRGINIA	Deer Run (Municipal), Newport News (1986)
WEST VIRGINIA	Oglebay Park, Wheeling (2000)
BELGIUM	Puyenbroek GC (2005)
DENMARK	Royal Golf Club, Copenhagen (2010) Rungsted Golf Club, Rungsted Kyst (2005) Kokkedal Golfklub, Horsholm (2018)

IRELAND	Old Head Golf Links, Kinsale Co. Cork
	    (1996–Present)
	Dromoland G&CC, County Claire (2003)
	Killeen Castle Golf Development,
	    County Meath (2001)
	Charles Land, Dublin (2004)
	Greystone GC, Dublin (2003)
	Stackstown GC, Dublin (2005)
	Old Head Golf Links, Kinsale Co. Cork –
	    No. 8 (2018)

Old Head Golf Links, Kinsale Co. Cork –
No. 10 (2019)

ITALY
San Lorenzo Resort, Dolomites (2012)

PHILIPPINES
Wack Wack G&CC (East Course),
Manilla (1979)

SPAIN
Las Melonares Golf Development (2005)
Maspalomas, Caneria (2005)
Maspalomas GC (2005)
Maspalomas Gran Caneria (2003)
Salobre GC (2005)
Lanzarote GC – New Course (2006)
Fuerteventura – New Course (2005)
Escorpion GC, Valencia (2016)

BARBADOS
Apes Hill Golf Club (2019)

RON KIRBY JOINED JACK NICKLAUS GOLF DESIGN SERVICES IN 1986 AND WAS RESPONSIBLE FOR THE FOLLOWING EUROPEAN PROJECTS

AUSTRIA   Gut Altenan, Salzburg

ENGLAND   Collingtree Park, Northhampton
                  London Golf Club, Seven Oaks

FRANCE   Cely GC, Cely
                  Paris International, Paris

IRELAND   Mt. Juliet Resort, Kilkenny

SCOTLAND   Gleneagles Hotel, Perthshire

SPAIN   La Moraleja, Madrid